POSTSCRIPT

by

BARRY SMITH

POSTSCRIPT

BY

BARRY SMITH

PUBLISHED BY
BARRY SMITH FAMILY EVANGELISM

ISBN 0-908961-04-9

TYPESET, PRINTED AND BOUND BY WRIGHT & CARMAN LTD
UPPER HUTT, NEW ZEALAND

CONTENTS

Communism not dead — FEMA — Privatisation — South Africa — Divide and rule — Aids created by man — Population control — Energy control — Food control — Oxygen therapy — Nuclear scam — New World Order — New Zealand guinea-pig nation — Japanese real estate collapse — N.Z. role model for Australia.

George Bush's Gulf War speech — Global 2000 — N.Z. Frontline documentary — Strange seal on U.S. dollar — Illuminati — Skull and Bones — Yale's Motto — Novus Ordo Seclorum — U.S. two groups — Secret Masonic information — Masonic symbols in Washington's streets — Inverted pentagram — Mason's say "Lucifer is God" — The Phoenix — Babel repeated — The Order — Kant and Hegal — Gulf War conflict introduced N.W.O. — Sovereignty of U.S. undermined — U.S. Presidents chosen, not elected — Conditionalities policies — International treaties — Parliamentarians redundant — Why N.Z. was chosen as a Guinea-pig nation.

ACKNOWLEDGEMENTS

Special thanks

To my dear wife **May**, for her love and patience and unsurpassed care as my help-meet — whether at home or travelling world-wide.

To my dear mother, **Vera** Smith, who celebrated her 86th birthday on the 17th June 1992. My Dad **Ted**, and Mum, helped me by bringing me up in the ways of the Lord. Thank you.

To my administrator son **Andrew**, and to our daughter-in-law **Saskia**, for the hours spent organising our tours and producing annointed music.

To my son-in-law **Dennie** Capell, for keeping our evangelistic vehicles on the road and to his wife, our eldest daughter **Becky**, for typing out the manuscript for this book.

To my son-in-law **Johnie** Koutsimanis and his wife, my second daughter **Rachel**, for the fine work they are doing in editing our monthly prophetic newspaper, the "Omega Times".

To my youngest daughter **Debbie** who is always there to help me in the many and varied projects connected with our ministry. God bless you Debbie.

To **Keith** and **Angela** Jones, our intrepid office staff who gave up much to assist in this valuable work for the Lord. We thank you.

To **Daniel Sarantidis** from Adelaide, South Australia, for the very clear illustration work, done at such short notice. Much appreciated.

To **Nic and Wendy Venter** for assisting, not only with our South African bookings, but also with the art work on the cover of this book.

NOSTRADAMUS —
EAT YOUR HEART OUT!

Written 20th June 1992

Did you know that nuclear devices cannot be set off at any time or at any place?

Is it true that there is an ozone problem?
Is there really such a thing as "Global Warming"?
Did you know that Aids was created in a laboratory?
Do you appear to have less money than you used to have?
Are you in danger of losing your job?
Do you wonder why politicians never appear to tell the truth?
Do you understand George Bush's New World Order?
Are you mystifed by the strange changes taking place around you?
Three nations will be withdrawn from the European Community.

STOP PRESS!

With reference to the peace negotiations going on in the **Middle East** between the Israelis and the Arabs, the ancient prophecies make it quite clear:

(a) **There will be a peace treaty signed shortly**.

The Israeli elections are over. Mr Rabin is the new Prime Minister, and he is in favour of the **land for peace deal** with the Arabs (24 June 1992.)

"Press", 3rd September 1992: The Palestinian spokeswoman said ". . . the Palestinian ten point framework was based on a document submitted in an earlier round but 'of course with modifications and taking into account some of the Israeli concerns and proposals'.

She listed the points as:

The nature of the self-government arrangements, stating that they are transitional for a five-year interim period while a final settlement is negotiated. . . ." End quote.

(b)   This peace treaty that we are watching for will be for a period of 7 years.

Dr Henry Kissinger being interviewed on CNN during the year 1992, made some interesting observations. He believes that INTERIM ARRANGEMENTS WILL BE SET IN PLACE TO LAST FOR 5-7 YEARS.

He spoke of 4 stages being fulfilled in these negotiations:

(a)   A period of optimism
(b)   A period of pessimism
(c)   "We will not let the talks collapse", he said "but will narrow the differences".
(d)   "WE will step in."

It is obvious to all who speak the English language that the word WE, always includes the speaker.

1992 U.S. Elections

Q. Why did the NWO people sack George Bush?
A. He had served his purpose in introducing the NWO and was looking aged and stressed out.
Q. Why was Bill Clinton chosen?
A. He is younger and fitter to carry on the task of undermining U.S. independence and taking that country into the Global Village.
Q. Is he a One World Government Man?
A. Very much so and has been thoroughly trained for the task. A Rhodes Scholar and Bilderbergers man.
Q. What will happen to him if he displeases his new bosses?
A. Ask Jack Kennedy. There is always the OAITCCT (ie The old arsenic in the coffee cup trick!).

x

Q. What would happen then?

A. Al Gore may come in, and he is absolutely dedicated to and gives lectures on New Age principles.

Q. Why is the U.S. presidential system so corrupt?

A. It must needs be. Please turn briefly to p. 22 and observe the map of Washington D.C. Please note the Satanic, inverted 5 pointed star (pentagram) built in the form of streets with the apex stopping right at the White House. A thorough reading of that section will answer your question.

By the way, your argument that none of this is possible is at this stage in history, irrelevant, to say the least. Please humble yourself and learn.

Q. Are there any other reasons for the choice of Clinton?

A. Yes. The Democrats were in power when the Camp David Treaty was signed on behalf of Egypt and Israel.

Many of the same advisors are waiting in the wings.

One of the advisors is Antichrist.

Proof

Jerusalem Post Nov. 1992

Quote — **"Republicans are already undermining Bill Clinton with foreign diplomats and businessmen . . .**

The hits come from former officials who have worked intimately with foreigners in 20 of the last 24 years and have gained their trust.

The underminers include the likes of Henry Kissinger . . .

This governor of a small southern state is dangerously inexperienced . . ." End quote.

In other words, Kissinger and co are saying, "Bill, you need our assistance with your foreign policy, particularly in the Middle East".

Q. Is there any real difference then between the Democrat and the Republican policies?

A. Not at all. Bill Bush and George Clinton both have the same bosses.

THIS AUTHOR'S BOOKS ARE FOR YOU!

by
Barry R. Smith

PREFACE

The author of this book, Barry Smith, is possibly one of the very few in the world today who could be called an "authority" on the "Global Plan" now being set up.

Those who are initiating this plan have boasted that not one in a million could possibly follow the maze that they have set up to throw people off the trail.

This author is that one in a million!

As a New Zealand citizen, he realised that his country had become a "test case" for massive changes that were ultimately to take place world wide.

This man has written three other books packed full of exciting information and this booklet is designed to bring you up-to-date with things you may expect during 1992 and beyond.

FOREWORD

The atmosphere was electric in the big tent. The speaker had just challenged the martial arts experts to step forward so that he could demonstrate a power greater than their own.

My cousin Derek Jones and I sat on a haybale situated right in the front so we didn't miss a thing.

Suddenly, the swearing and cursing started and a group representing the martial arts teachers, led by a top black belt exponent, began marching down the aisle between the hay-bales.

"Come on. Don't you swear at me. Come up here and I'll show you something," taunted the speaker.

I turned to Derek and murmured "He's really overdone it this time", indicating that we had better get ready to give him a hand.

The karate expert and his entourage had by this time reached the front and surrounded the speaker, who continued on with his message, apparently oblivious to all that was taking place.

The owner of the black-belt drew back his hand and with a loud cry from his lips "Ahhhhhh", prepared for the coup de gras karate chop. . . . The packed crowd in the tent steeled themselves for the violent scene about to be enacted, when all of a sudden, to everyone's amazement, the black belt's hands appeared absolutely powerless as he swung numerous blows — not only powerless, but at point blank range not one blow connected. A look of confusion and embarrassment came over his face as he gripped that arm with his other hand and bolted for the exit flap. His group, all looking extremely foolish, ran after him into the darkness, whilst those remaining in the tent erupted into a frenzy of shouting, clapping and cheering.

The speaker, (**Barry Smith**), continued on as though nothing had happened.

The venue — Nambassa Rock Festival, held on a farm south of Auckland, New Zealand.

Living with my father, the speaker, my mother May and my three sisters — Becky, Rachel and Deborah, has been very exciting at times.

Some have described his statements on occasions to be "over the top", or even "outrageous", but often, as time goes by, many of these same critics confess, "My word, he was right!" I have read many letters outlining this fact.

I hereby invite you, the reader to turn the pages in this

book and understand that this world is indeed in the hands of the evil one. Many people I speak with cannot handle the concept of conspiracies and mass manipulation of humans by minority groups. You may prefer to believe, as new age philosophers teach, that "men are basically good and we just need to tap into the good side of our natures to unleash a being of pure selfless motivation. . . ." RIDICULOUS!

Sometime ago, my wife and I went to have a look at a house we were interested in. We had only just met the owner of the dwelling when she began to pour out a list of personal grievances she had recently experienced. At the centre of her sad tale was her separation from her de facto partner who had run off with another woman. Apparently, the relationship of around six years had been stable enough. This lady was speaking about her situation as if an injustice had happened. I empathised with her in her hurt and loneliness but had to say something that I knew she wouldn't want to hear.

I began, "Who says it's unlawful for your partner to do what he's doing? Who sets the standard in your life that tells you some things are wrong and other things are right?"

In other words, this lady had presented a case of injustice founded upon "nothing". Where was the injustice, because where was the standard which said that her partner was doing wrong?

She ignored me, continuing on with her story of hurt and mistreatment. Again I had to speak, "Hang on a minute. Unless you have a standard to which you are both committed, all you are trusting in in this relationship is man's natural inborn goodness".

Basically we have only two options. The first is to live life hanging on to the hope that mans' "natural inborn goodness" is able to overcome inherent selfishness and greed. That the "golden rule" (do unto others . . .) may become an invisible standard allowing people to live together happily to a ripe old age . . .

OR

to accept the fact that all of us need to be liberated from a prison of self-centredness. We need also to realise that a man can only be truly honourable when he is in harmony and correct relationship with a spiritual power greater than himself.

Who is the ruling power in your life?

May this book help you with that decision.

Andrew E. Smith
Administrator for International Support Ministries – Pacific

PART ONE

THINGS ARE NOT ALWAYS AS THEY SEEM

(1) Communism has not collapsed. It is simply restructuring and has never given up its avowed aim of ruling the world.

Their philosophy has always been "If the iron fist fails, try the velvet glove approach."

During the month of July 1992, a Christian preacher friend of mine, whilst on a tour of Russia, was interviewed by the KGB for four and a half hours. When I heard this, I said to him, "Strange, I thought communism had collapsed". He laughingly replied "Tell that to the Russians".

Those of us involved in prophecy are very clear in our minds that soon after a seven year peace treaty has been signed in the Middle East, Russia and many other nations will invade Israel.

At this time of writing, please notice that there is no mention in the media about a peace treaty being only seven years in length. This is hidden knowledge revealed only in prophecy.

(2) The Rodney King beating and subsequent calling in of the National Guard to subdue rioters — could this be a prelude to a complete takeover in the U.S.?

1

As soon as the news broke that the thugs who beat Rodney King were to be acquitted, I received a telephone call from California advising me that this calling in of the National Guard to quell the riots was possibly a foretaste of FEMA (Federal Emergency Management Act). Readers will be surprised to learn that in the case of a national emergency, the President of the U.S. has the authority to take over the complete running of the country and thus overrule the Constitution of United States of America.

During the Iran Contra scandal, Colonel Oliver North was asked by the then Texas senator whether he at any time had been involved in a plan to suspend the Constitution of the United States. He was about to answer when the Chairman of the investigating committee, the senator from Hawaii, said, "This is a matter of national security and will not be answered in open session but will be dealt with privately later."

May and I were visiting Great Britain during the year 1990 and were fortunate enough to view the above information portrayed clearly on British television. This is not a story from a friend of a friend of a friend.

Obviously, for the New World Order to include the United States of America, the founding document of that country, the Constitution, must be overruled.

(3) **The average citizen will realise too late that privatisation** means the selling up of his nation's sovereignty. In future then, when you see this word "privatising", remember that it simply means that the object of this privatisation is about to be sold overseas to the New World Order people. Goodbye sovereignty of New Zealand, Australia, U.S.A., Canada, South Africa and every country in the world.

Clever, isn't it!

SOUTH AFRICA

It has been the privilege of my wife and I to visit this great country on two occasions and to lecture in all its major cities on the subject of the New World Order.

Only those who spend time here understand the massive problems being encountered in this area of the world.

Under the N.W.O., each country has been singled out for one major product or industry which will make it very important in the context of a **Global Village** e.g.

New Zealand — Pine Trees

Australia — Wheat

South Africa — Minerals

Can you see how that other industries are being decimated and being made obsolete.

The aim of all this apparent confusion is clear. Wars are supposed to become outmoded in the future as we all need each other in order to survive.

Now, in South Africa, there are so many factions, that the New World Order organisers have to infiltrate this country in a very special way.

It is called **"Divide and Rule"**.

Henry Kissinger, some years ago, drawing on the ideas of three great politicians in European history i.e. Castlereagh, Metternich and Bismarck, borrowed two phrases of great significance.

"A Global Concept" — This means no small nation is any longer important by itself. The world must in future be viewed as a globe, a unity and as a whole.

"The Balance of Power" — This means the nations of the earth must not be allowed to be perfectly at peace but must undergo constant agitation to keep them on the

3

balance of war and peace until the NWO's nefarious schemes have been perfected.

Now, South Africa is a case in point.

The NWO people work more easily with Communist governments and this is why much of the rest of Africa has been allowed to, in fact, some may say encouraged to, install communist governments.

These in turn soon become so impoverished under these governments that they become easy pickings for the NWO people and their plans.

The tension in South Africa during our 1992 tour had to be experienced to be believed.

MAIN PARTIES

(a)   The many black indigenous groups
(b)   The right wing white minority armed to the teeth
(c)   The white South Africans, from English or Afrikaaner stock
(d)   The white government of the day
(e)   The black groups clamouring to be the government

(It should be noted by the reader that the vast majority of these dear people wish only to live in peace.)

Sadly, just prior to leaving this great country, we read an extraordinary article in the local Johannesburg newspaper, revealing the presence of **a highly secret 3rd force.**

"Johannesburg Star", 25th August 1992: "A former senior military intelligence officer is talking and the scenario he sketches of a 'third force' operating here and now in South Africa is chilling. . . .

Colonel . . . states as a fact that security force-linked operatives have been actively stoking the political violence which has claimed 7000 lives in the past two years.

"Some of the attacks — some of the train massacres, for example — bear the unmistakable hallmarks of the Special Forces reconnaissance regiments. . . .

Escalating 'black-on-black' killings — particularly involving the ANC and the Inkatha Freedom Party — have been 'a dream come true' for 'third force' practitioners. . . ." End quote.

This group is alleged to be keeping the pot boiling by stirring up township violence, resulting in shootings, hackings, spearings and necklacings.

The outside world reads about all this and says "Ho hum", yet we have spoken to some of these dear folk who live in the townships, and have empathised with them in the terror which continually surrounds them. A knock at the door in the middle of the night can mean death within five seconds.

Violence is so bad in this country that the following article from the Johannesburg Star should boggle the mind. Dated 20th July 1992, "Unexpected crime drop encouraging.

Police are encouraged by an unexpected drop in crime — **'only' 59,978 people were arrested for serious crimes last month"**. End quote.

Those with strong spiritual values can now see that South Africa's only hope is a massive spiritual revival which the prophets have promised **will** take place.

Isaiah 59:19b — "When the enemy shall come in like a flood, the spirit of the Lord shall lift up a standard against him."

In the midst of all this apparent confusion, **South Africa**, along with the rest of the world, is **privatising** and selling out to overseas investors.

A recent cutting from the Post Courier newspaper, **Papua New Guinea**, 12th August 1992, reads: "Government gets okay to privatise.

The government has taken the first step towards **privatising** State-run commercial statutory bodies." End quote.

On the 9th July 1992, whilst visiting the island of **Mauritius** in the Indian Ocean, May and I were walking around town in Port Louis, when we came across a very noisy demonstration conducted in the French language.

We understood clearly by the words on the placards that they were endeavouring to stop the **privatising** of some of their larger firms. Many of these signs read "Non privatisation".

The news is getting out. These workers obviously saw the end result of privatisation as not only loss of jobs, but loss of sovereignty.

AIDS CREATED BY MAN

(4) The newspapers in Australia and New Zealand are confirming that the AIDS virus did not come from the Green Monkey in Africa. Many experts say it was created in a laboratory by combining two deadly retroviruses i.e. the bovine leukaemia virus from the cow — (BLV), and the visna virus from the sheep. The BLV is present in dairy herds in New Zealand and other countries. The newspapers are reporting that the belief is that the virus was

**imported into our country through Friesian cows
and has been spread through vaccinations using
the same needle on each cow.**

"New Zealand Herald", 28th June 1991: "Bovine Aids
virus common in NZ herds". "A cattle virus similar to
Aids and capable of crossing into other species has
appeared in New Zealand herds. Bovine
immunodeficiency virus (BIV) is already being labelled
Cow Aids in the United States . . .

. . . the close similiarities had led to the creation of a large
project in Ames, Iowa, to investigate BIV as a potential
model for the study of Aids. . . ." End quote.

In an article entitled "Biological Warfare" (J. Roy Soc.
Med. — 1986, Aug. 79 494) we read: "Moscow Radio has
reportedly drawn attention to a British researcher's
'conclusion' that the AIDS virus has been artificially
created, its appearance the result of a human error during
human experiments carried out by the USA as part of
the development of new biological weapons.

. . . there is ample evidence to believe that such an
operation has been carried out at a secret American
laboratory.

. . . Transmission modes are highly suggestive of a man-
made virus produced by passage of an animal virus in
vitro through human tissue culture then in vivo through
humans used as guinea pigs. . . .

. . . the virus was not necessarily created by military
scientists, and could just as easily have originated in
Russian laboratories to be released on an unsuspecting
West." End quote.

Two brave doctors in the U.S.A., Dr Strecker and Dr
Douglass, have studied and researched this question in

great depth and it is now possible to link the creation of the AIDS virus to the World Government plan for world population control. Over 2 billion people have been targeted for annihilation, then with a smaller population, diminished food resources will control the remainder.

You owe it to yourself to also purchase the video tape called **The Strecker Memorandum**, available from THE STRECKER GROUP, 1501 Colorado Blvd, Eagle Rock, CA 90041, U.S.A. Ph: (213) 344-8039.

This information on the origin of AIDS is absolutely mind-boggling and has been researched by a very brave man.

Readers of our previous book will know that the New World Order people have a number of cliches which describe their diabolical plans e.g.

BY CONTROLLING ENERGY,
WE CAN CONTROL NATIONS
BY CONTROLLING FOOD,
WE CAN CONTROL PEOPLE

An update on this information is presented herewith.

a. Farming has been so decimated in the guinea pig country of New Zealand that many farms are greatly depleted of livestock. Unpredictable weather patterns have also played a part in all this and thus caught the N.W.O. planners unawares.

b. In Australia, many farmers have dug giant holes in the ground with their bull-dozers and have been forced to shoot millions of sheep. I remember watching a programme on television where one of these farmers, with a gun in his hand, was interviewed. He said "If the Prime Minister was here with us today, I have reserved a bullet for him."

c. The latest news to hand from Australia is that in the Northern Territory and north Queensland, helicopters are flying on regular missions with hunters shooting thousands and thousands of cattle beasts which, the authorities claim, have been infected with TB. One such farmer in that area has lost over 2 million dollars in stock already.

We hope all this is clear —

a. Cut down on the food supplies
b. Cut down on the world population
c. Control those who are left through deceptive food distribution. (For those who study the prophecies, please remember the rider on the black horse with scales in his hand — see Revelation 6:8.)

HYPER-OXYGENATION THERAPY

At last, there is hope for AIDS and cancer patients! We at this office are very concerned that the news on this subject is not being promoted by the media. Having just returned from a tour of Africa, my wife and I have observed first hand the horror and the devastation of this terrible man-made condition.

We read that the cure is so simple and inexpensive that the medical authorities in most countries merely ignore the very subject and do not even bother to research it as there is no money to be made from it.

We are being told that aids and cancer is being controlled in certain parts of Mexico and Germany by using Oxygen Therapy i.e. $H2O2 - 35\%$ food grade or Ozone. Please note — **This therapy is to be administered only by trained medical specialists.** (Please refer to addresses listed in the back of this book.)

For example, Dr Rokistansky, a Vienna surgeon, is one of the leaders in ozone therapy in Europe. He and other physicians often flow ozone gas over open lesions such as diabetic gangrene on feet, hands, arms or legs. The ozone eliminates any need for amputation of the extremity.

Other doctors treat cancer sucessfully with ozone.

We trust that medical doctors world-wide will hear this information and in their love for their fellow man, defy the drug companies and research this form of inexpensive healing.

NUCLEAR SCAM

(5) **Since I wrote chapter 14 (page 92) in my book "Final Notice", regarding the Nuclear Con, readers may have noticed that there is now a concentrated world-wide effort to apparently cut back on nuclear arsenals.**

The reason for this is clear to us. The psychological scare tactics have already done their job and have terrified the uninformed populations of each country into seeking a remedy to this apparent problem. Although there never was a problem, these master schemers are now promoting a media blitz to show that nuclear deterrents are no longer necessary and the average reader of the world's newspapers has gone along and swallowed the story hook, line and sinker.

There will not, because there cannot ever be, a nuclear war! It can be proven that nuclear devices are not too difficult to build, but can only be triggered through the spacial relationship of the sun and the earth at a given instant of time.

10

Each nation's top scientists know this highly-secret fact and exactly when and where such a detonation could take place. This will explain to you why no terrorist ever threatens to use nuclear weapons. Our office is continually being contacted by physics specialists and would-be scientists who tell me that what I wrote on this subject in my book 'Final Notice' is not correct.

I would point out in a kindly manner that the information on the detonation of a nuclear device has been **"doctored"** at the universities, and that any who wish to pursue this matter may do so by taking note of the timing of the nuclear detonations at Mururoa Atoll, then by using their sun tables, check out the position of the sun in relation to the earth each time one of these devices was detonated.

Some have already done this. One scientist, for example, argued with a friend of mine for a period of sixteen hours and finally exclaimed "My word, you're right. By simply changing a plus to a minus in the equation, your point may be proven correct."

With this in mind, you can now see there will never be a nuclear war and New Zealand's "nuclear free" policy is a complete waste of time.

We invite any reader, or group of readers skilled in mathematics, to purchase a copy of Bruce Cathie's book, "The Energy Grid", (for address see back of book), buy a set of sun tables and do their own calculations working backwards from any nuclear test conducted at Mururoa Atoll in the Pacific, or the Nevada test site in the U.S.A.

(6) **The words "New World Order" are not new. They have been written on the reverse side of every $1.00 U.S. bill since the year 1933.**

Mikhail Gorbachev from Russia has at last said publicly what we we have been saying for years. Quote — "The

11

need for some kind of 'global government' is gaining ground. . . ." End quote.

The words "New World Order" mean simply — A Godless, One World Government.

(7) The little country of New Zealand, for a number of reasons, has been chosen as the GUINEA PIG NATION for the New World Order.

The President of the World Bank made this very clear when he visited New Zealand in the late 1980's.

Quote — "New Zealand's economic restructuring was a ROLE MODEL for other countries which also had to adjust their policies to achieve growth."

On the 24th April 1991, New Zealand's minister of Finance gave a budget speech in which that country's welfare state underwent massive cuts. On a programme entitled "Business Hour", on that date, it was revealed that this speech was televised and viewed with interest in the financial capitals of the world. Why? Because New Zealand, as it was explained, was the ROLE MODEL for handling the 'welfare state'. (See also chapter 21 in our book 'Final Notice'.)

Look at this — New Zealand Herald, 17th August 1991. Quote —

"Guinea pig tactic with economy condemned.

New Zealanders are being used as GUINEA PIGS to test an economic theory which the governnment seems determined to pursue even though it is obvious it cannot work. . . ." End quote.

The man quoted in the passage above, should know what he is talking about, as he is a University PROFESSOR OF ECONOMICS in the "test case" country of New Zealand.

He continues on — "We are really looking at the old saying 'The operation was a success but the patient died . . .' Referring to the government he says 'They are either missing the point, or hiding it . . . or both . . .'" End quote.

(8) The New World Order will be introduced through a Japanese real estate collapse, and the 'New International Economic Order' will be introduced.

From the Herald-Sun Business page in Australia, 10th April 1992, we read the headline: "Collapse of Japan will bring New World Order." End quote.

It has been said that the value of the real-estate 300 square kilometres south of Tokyo is equal to the real estate value of a large portion of the United States of America. The crash, set off either by an earthquake or stock market collapse will:

(a) devalue the yen
(b) crash the U.S. dollar
(c) crash the German mark
(d) crash the whole world economy

It is obvious to all who study these matters that stage one is almost complete with the shaky Japanese economy, therefore, stage two will then be introduced — a plastic card, complete with at least seven problems which are explained further on.

The ancient prophecy now applies. A future world leader will ultimately make sure the future trading mark is placed under the skin on either the right hand or the forehead.

Revelation 13:16-18: "And he causeth all, both small and great, rich and poor, free and bond, to receive a mark in their right hand, or in their foreheads:

And that no man might buy or sell, save he that had the mark, or the name of the beast, or the number of his name. Here is wisdom. Let him that hath understanding count the number of the beast: for it is the number of a man; and his number is Six hundred threescore and six."

Remember now, that New Zealand is the world's first in the setting up of this New World Order. Its near neighbour, Australia, is second on the list. This author and his wife know this to be true because we spend much of our time between both of these countries. Electronic Funds Transfer — EFT on a national basis was announced as "The World's First" by the Westpac Bank in Australia in 1984.

In the Christchurch Press on the 24th June 1992, we read the headline "Australia's political debate focuses on NZ experience. New Zealand has a particular place in the Australian political debate because many of the changes that the Liberal Party, the senior member of the coalition, plans to introduce into Australia, if it wins the next election, are already in place in New Zealand. **This country has become both the model and the laboratory.** A large number of Liberal politicians have visited New Zealand during the last few years to study how the changes were introduced and what the effect has been.

Broadly speaking, the argument in Australia is the same argument which occurred in New Zealand — that of the free market as opposed to the regulated market. In particular the coalition plans **a goods and services tax** and **to introduce industrial changes modelled on the Employment Contracts Act.**" End quote.

All this means, in simple English, as New Zealanders have watched their country being wrecked, get ready Australians, yours is next on the list.

PART TWO

AMAZING SECRETS REVEALED

We were visiting our daughter Rachel, her husband Yanni and the grand-children. The situation in the Gulf was explosive and that very afternoon I heard Yanni call out "Dad, come inside — George Bush is speaking on television and is announcing an attack on Saddam Hussein's Iraq."

As the whole of our family watched President Bush on the television screen, I rose to my feet and shouted **"COME ON GEORGE, SAY THE WORDS, SAY THE WORDS."**

15

I had barely finished my call when he responded with the phrase **"WORLD ORDER"**, then later, a second time **"NEW WORLD ORDER"**, and then still later, he used a very obscure phrase, referring to **"A THOUSAND POINTS OF LIGHT."**

NEW WORLD ORDER is a coded language meaning a One World Government.

A THOUSAND POINTS OF LIGHT means that there are about one thousand Illuminated Satanic groups who are bringing this World Government about. (Please also note that the NWO people will have a completely innocent explanation for this peculiar phrase.)

My whole family rose to their feet, clapped and cheered as this is "my subject". Therefore, if you think you personally can name one group responsible for these massive changes taking place on the earth today, there are probably 999 other groups that you do **not** know about.

(Please note, each phrase of relevance will commence with the word — FACT. This author holds all the back-up material necessary to prove every point he makes.)

FACT 1 — George Bush's "NEW WORLD ORDER" was initially introduced by Jimmy Carter's plan entitled "GLOBAL 2000." This means that the individuals belonging to these 1000 groups have set the year 2000 as the key year when all should be under way in the creation of a ONE WORLD GOVERNMENT.

Whilst speaking on these subjects in Australia during the year 1990, I was approached by a business couple who told me an amazing story.

A lady had come into their shop introducing herself as belonging to a group called "2000". She made it quite clear to them both that they should sign on the dotted line, thus associating themselves with this group who promised that if they did, their business would continue to succeed and if, on the other hand, they didn't sign, their business would not continue to succeed.

The couple were naturally very upset as this sounded to them like a modern version of "Mafia protection".

They refused the offer and the lady concerned used their telephone to call her superior. They heard her say words to this effect, "They will not sign. Strike their name from the register."

The couple later revealed to me that until they heard the information so clearly presented on the New World Order, this incident did not make any sense, but at that stage, everything became very clear.

FACT 2 — Many of these groups and individuals are not consciously evil but sincere in their efforts to undermine national governments and their sovereignty. These countries in financial, social and ecological desperation, will then yield to the World Body which is supported by many groups including the Council on Foreign Relations, Bilderbergers, Club of Rome, Trilateral Commission, New Age Movement, Round Table, the Upper Degrees in Freemasonry, Rockefellers, Rothschilds etc, etc.

NEW ZEALAND

A media group called "Frontline" in New Zealand presented a very powerful documentary suggesting very strongly that big business was controlling the government of this guinea pig nation New Zealand. This documentary was not allowed to be shown in New Zealand but the Australian media presented it to their public.

This author was sent a copy of that video tape and can now understand why the reporters involved were sacked from the programme and why certain politicians were breathing fire and threatening libel charges.

Political Rules—When under pressure in any adverse way, attack vehemently and intimidate those not protected by parliamentary privilege.

Sequel to the above.

During the month of June 1992, a New Zealand government politician began to stir the pot again by suggesting that big business was possibly involved in underhand dealings with the government. There was even talk of a second television programme being filmed revealing details of the suspected corruption.

The Sunday Star, 14th June 1992, revealed that a university sociology lecturer sat next to a man on a plane travelling from Sydney to Canberra on April 23rd 1992. This other man "spent the flight going through a document marked 'strictly confidential' . . . (the lecturer) told the Government MP . . . what he had seen. He said the paper suggested **damage limitation** . . .

The first damage control measure would be silence from the main parties in the hope the allegations would disappear.

If that failed, the next step would be statements from business people and politicians calling for evidence to support the allegations.

If that failed, phase 3 would be a diversionary campaign, focusing on personalities and attacking the credibility of those making allegations.

If that failed, the main parties should go to ground . . ." End quote.

It is no wonder then that at the time of writing this same MP is under tremendous pressure from both his government colleagues and big business. He is a brave man indeed!

FACT 3 — The term NEW WORLD ORDER is spoken of by a number of people including George Bush, Mikhail Gorbachev, Henry Kissinger, Bob Hawke, and members of many government groups.

The words NOVUS ORDO SECLORUM are found on the strange seal on the reverse side of every post 1933 US$1.00 bill.

The meaning of this phrase written in Latin is "A completely Godless (heathenistic) New World Order".

Novus — new

Ordo — order

Seclorum — Godless or heathenistic

No wonder born-again committed Christians are being persecuted in many parts of the world. The New Age movement in particular does not disguise the fact that one of its aims is to get rid of God's people as soon as possible, as they are a thorn in the flesh to harmonisation with other religious bodies.

Readers of our previous books we trust will be aware of the beginnings of this world government plan.

Illuminati — Adam Weishaupt, May 1st 1776 (please refer to the Encyclopaedia Brittanica)

Baron Von Knigge — 1778, infiltrated Masonic Lodges in the upper degrees (please refer to the Encyclopaedia Brittanica, an older version, as this information has now been deleted.)

Complaints regarding this information should be addressed, not to our office, but to the Editor of the Encyclopaedia Brittanica.

FACT 4 — Whilst at Yale University, both George Bush and his father before him belonged to a very highly secret fraternity which has its roots in Germany i.e. The Skull and Bones or 322. Upon leaving Yale, its members go on to become "the Order", a group dedicated to encouraging all nations to yield up their national sovereignty, along with their independence. These nations then become part of a world community called a GLOBAL VILLAGE in which every country in the world assists all other countries through INTERDEPENDENCE.

FACT 5 — President George Bush of course, would be aware of the motto of Yale University. That motto is written in Latin and is exactly the same phrase that one may read on the reverse side of every American $1.00 bill —
i.e. Novus Ordo Seclorum.

20

FACT 6 — The United States of America was settled by **two main groups**.

(a) **The Pilgrim Fathers** — their aims, religious freedom.

My wife May and I were thrilled to visit Plymouth Ho in Southern England during the year 1990. Down at the wharf, we observed a brass plate which was placed there as being the very spot where the Pilgrim Fathers waved farewell to Mother England. We viewed the green fields, the water, and the harbour entrance and our minds went back more than two hundred years to that little group who saw similar scenes as they sailed out into destiny.

(b) **Occultists and Freemasons** — their aims, to set Lucifer (or Satan) on the throne of the world.

Proof — A top Masonic writer called Manly Hall, states much of this information quite openly in his book entitled "THE SECRET TEACHINGS OF ALL AGES". (If this information upsets you, please don't become angry with me. Contact Mr Hall.)

Quote: "Not only were many of the founders of the United States Government Masons, **but they received aid from a secret and august body existing in Europe, which helped them to establish this country for: A PECULIAR AND PARTICULAR PURPOSE KNOWN ONLY TO THE INITIATED FEW**. (Capitals added for emphasis.) The Great Seal is the signature of this exalted body — unseen and for the most part unknown — and the unfinished pyramid upon its reverse side is a trestleboard, setting forth symbolically the task to the accomplishment of which THE UNITED STATES GOVERNMENT WAS DEDICATED FROM THE DAY OF ITS INCEPTION . . ." (Capitals added for emphasis) — End quote.

Author's note—It is now abundantly clear that the **PECULIAR AND PARTICULAR PURPOSE** is to be brought to fruition if possible by the year 2000. The name again—**"New World Order"** or "Global 2000".

Now, note this—the city of Washington D.C. was designed by these Freemasons. With your own eyes, you can now establish the accuracy of this statement.

The Masonic symbols i.e. the compass and square have been boldly and arrogantly built into the streets of this

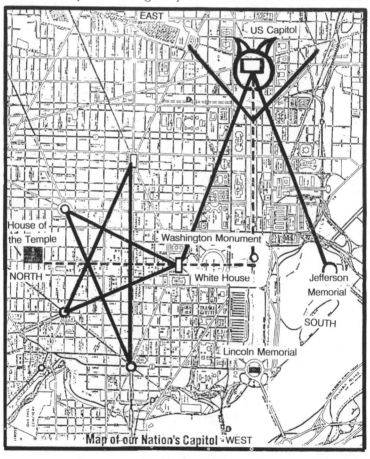

city. For a country, which for many years has adhered to the motto 'In God We Trust', I find this to be outrageous! Notice also the occultic pentagram which becomes a neighbour to the White House.

Please observe that the pentagram (or five pointed star) is inverted and in witchcraft, this stands for a very powerful demon named "Baphomet" and is signified by the goat's head inserted inside the pentagram. Careful observation will reveal the horns at the top, the ears at the sides and the beard at the bottom. This beard stops right at the White House, therefore, every president of the U.S.A. has had the devil right in his bedroom.

These masonic symbols i.e. the square, the compass and the pentagram are actual streets which conflict with the grid system on the map and we have coloured them in for clarity.

I showed this to a leading mason recently and he commented that it must have happened by accident.

Words fail me!

Readers of our book "Second Warning" will remember reading the section on Freemasonry and the quotation on page 96 where Albert Pike declares that "Lucifer is God".

Some masons that I have spoken to (a) deny that Albert Pike ever said this (b) claim that it was a plot by anti-masonic forces, printed to discredit Freemasonry (c) said that they had never heard of such a thing.

A 32nd degree man that I spoke to midway through the year 1992, claimed to be a born again Christian and told me that if I could show that Freemasonry was connected in any way to Lucifer, he would resign.

I quoted this story from the book "Second Warning" on page 96 where an Australian mason in the State of New South Wales explained to me that in the book of Revelation, Jesus Christ is referred to as the "bright and morning star". He also said that Lucifer is referred to in the book of Isaiah 14 as "son of the morning".

"Can't you see, Mr Smith", he said, "They are the same person".

"How dare you," I said. "Don't you speak to me again."

We have travelled worldwide telling this story and in the year 1988, the Freemasons wrote "A Response to Specific Criticisms of Freemasonry — Part Two" (The New South Wales Freemason, vol 20 no.5, February 1988).

NO EMOTION PLEASE

As we are dealing in simple facts, we will see what these men have to say for themselves.

Quote: "This is the second part of a response to specific criticisms of Freemasonry prepared by a Masonic Committee of Chaplains . . .

Criticism: Freemasonry is associated with the worship of the devil, and 'the all-seeing eye' is the eye of Satan.

No, even though certain people read such opinions into Masonic phrases and comments taken completely out of context. For example, they interpret the American scholar Pike's statement that some Masons refer to God as 'Lucifer' to be devil worship.

But, Lucifer, as Satan, occurs only in secular literature, originally in the imaginative mind of Milton's 'Paradise Lost'. Lucifer (Torchbearer) is the Roman god of the morning star, whose pre-dawn rising illumines the eastern sky.

In Revelation 22:16 we read, 'I Jesus, am the bright and morning star'. This means Jesus has identified Himself with the qualities of the morning star or Lucifer—a fitting title for Him whom Christians regard as the Light of the world.

Some Masonic degrees are restricted to Christians, whose members refer to God as 'Jesus', or as Pike stated, 'Lucifer'.

Critics offer no proof that the all-seeing eye is the eye of Satan. Had they consulted any concordance, they would have found references like, 'the eyes of the Lord, which run to and fro through the whole earth' (Zachariah (sic) 4:10; 2 Cronicles (sic) 16:9). Only in that context do Masons refer to the all-seeing eye—a necessary reminder that the eyes of the Lord are always upon us." End quote.

Author's comments—

(a) I would recommend that the Committee of Chaplains spend more time reading the Bible and try and get the spelling of Zechariah and Chronicles correct.

(b) The living God that we serve is the God of Abraham, Isaac and Jacob, the Father of our Lord Jesus Christ. He does not have ONE eye, and it is certainly not in a triangle. Anybody into the occult understands the secret power of the symbol within the triangle.

(c) Satan worshippers and those involved in delivering people from demonic spirits, know perfectly well that Lucifer was thrown out of heaven. **This degrading experience certainly never happened to our Lord Jesus Christ.**

Isaiah 14:12—"How art thou fallen from heaven O Lucifer, son of the morning! how art thou cut down to the ground, which didst weaken the nations!

26

For thou hast said in thine heart . . . I will be like the most High.
Yet thou shalt be brought down to the hell, to the sides of the pit."

Lucifer is now called "Satan" or the god of this world. You have just read where he is going, and you will go there also if you continue to belong to a group that calls this demonic being their god. Therefore, **Lucifer and Satan are the same being**!

(d) Anybody familiar with the Mormon Church will know that Joseph Smith and his brother Hiram were Freemasons, and were allowed the privilege of climbing up beyond the 30th degree in one day.

Is it any accident then that Mormon teaching makes Lucifer the brother of Jesus. Any person going through the temple rites in the Mormon Church will also observe the Masonic symbols of the square and compass on the veil.

(e) These so-called 'Chaplains' have blown their cover. At last, they have made it very clear and even written it down for all to see, that the names Jesus and Lucifer are interchangeable. Our very strong advice is now that we have shown you this **blasphemous information** from your own leaders' pens, you must resign immediately as your precious soul is in terrible danger of hell fire.

IRREFUTABLE PROOF FOR FREEMASONS

The author of this book, along with other Christian writers around the world, has spent hours and hours doing what you as a Freemason should have done before you joined this deceitful society.

Can you imagine joining something, and then finding out later that what you have joined is controlled by God's greatest enemy i.e. Lucifer (Satan).

Over the years I have met many Freemasons, including

those who have attained the so-called upper degrees e.g. 32nd degree. One such man had already been accepted for the 33rd degree and was proud of this fact.

The strange thing is, many men in the Blue Lodge, in the first, second or third degrees, do not know that there are other degrees above them.

Another strange thing is, that some men in the 32nd and 33rd degrees do not know that there are other degrees above them, leading on to the capstone which is Lucifer — the eye in the triangle on the reverse side of the American $1.00 bill.

When approached as to the Luciferian nature of this movement, all these men find it very difficult to hold their tongues, which is a pity, because they may learn something. In every case, they tend to rattle off the same old platitudes about the good deeds done by the Masons and the Masonic Lodges. Of course we know all this about the hospitals, widows, and old people's homes . . . but none of these is the point of our argument.

Instead of facing the truth of what we are telling them, they pick on tiny little differences that we have said take place in the lodges and argue that these things do not take place **in their particular lodge**.

Of course we know that each country has slight differences in their ritual . . . so therefore, this is irrelevant to the point of our argument.

They niggle over such words as "taking an oath" and tell us that they did not do this but "entered into an obligation".

Of course, we are adult enough to know that when one is dealing with spiritual matters, the devil behind these "oaths" or "obligations", is laughing in the background as his puppet denies the truth once more.

We present herewith, for the reader's information a spiritual pyramid for all Freemasons, their wives and families, to examine.

Lucifer:
"The Light of Limitless Nothingness"

T.G.A.O.T.U.
The "Seven"
The 9 "Unknown Men"
The "Illuminati"
The Palladium
Ordo Templi Orientis (O.T.O.)
Ancient & Primitive Rite (97 Degrees)
The Order of the Trapezoid
Supreme Council of Grand Sovereign Inspectors General
Grand Sovereign Inspectors General — 33rd Degree
(The Shrine)
Scottish Rite or York Rite Masonry
Blue Lodge Masonry

N.B. The first eight catagories descending from the top of the pyramid are European (Esoteric — privileged and secret) Masonry groups. The remainder are U.S. Masonry groups.

It would be fruitless at this point to argue that you do not belong to American Freemasonry. Again this is not the point.

To all Freemasons in every country, we state, "You are connected to a Luciferian society, whether you like it or not."

To any Mason reading this section, please take your pen and mark your level on this pyramid with a cross. (For further information, please purchase the following book "Masonry — Beyond The Light" by William Schnoebelen.

Published by Chick Publications, P.O. Box 662, Chino, CA 91708-0662, U.S.A.)

Mind-boggling information you will agree. Remember the phrase "STOP THE WORLD, I WANT TO GET OFF!!" This is not possible sorry, — read on.

FACT 7 — Now this piece of information will really upset U.S. citizens.

Manly Hall continues. Quote: "European mysticism was not dead at the time the United States of America was founded. The hand of the Mysteries CONTROLLED IN THE ESTABLISHMENT OF THE NEW GOVERN-MENT, (Capitals added for emphasis) for the signature of the Mysteries may still be seen on the Great Seal of the United States of America. Careful analysis of the seal discloses **a mass of occult and Masonic symbols**, chief

among them, the so-called **American eagle** . . . the American eagle upon the Great Seal is but a CONVENTIONALISED PHOENIX . . ." End quote.

What is a Phoenix? It's a mystical bird that rises out of the ashes. These ashes we know to be man's first attempt to set up a Luciferian or Satanic One World Government. This **first attempt** was called the building of the tower of Babel.

"So the Lord scattered them abroad from thence upon the face of the earth, and they left off to build the city. Therefore, the name of it is called Babel . . ." Genesis 11:8&9.

The first attempt failed and the Lord destroyed it, but this second attempt will succeed but for a very short season i.e. three and a half years in particular.

In a quote from the Melbourne Sun, Australia 16th May 1992, we read a remarkable statement. It is clear that Margaret Thatcher understands that this New World Order will be linked to the European Community which comes to power on the 31st December 1992. She also understands the Phoenix principle.

Quote — "Margaret Thatcher yesterday launched a scathing attack on the European Community saying it would not be strong enough to contain Germany.

. . . A reunited Germany can't and won't subordinate national interests in economic or in foreign policy of the community indefinitely, she said.

. . . Mrs Thatcher drew a picture of a 30 state E.C. led from Brussels, and with each state having the same work conditions, monetary and interests rates, policies and foreign policy . . ."

(The next paragraph boggled even this author's mind.) "Such an body is an even more utopian enterprise than

31

the TOWER OF BABEL. **AT LEAST THE BUILDERS OF BABEL ALL SPOKE THE SAME LANGUAGE WHEN THEY BEGAN**. (Emphasis added).

. . . She called centralised bureaucracy the wrong future for Europe . . ." End quote.

FACT 8 — The Order to which George Bush belongs is a German secret society which follows the philosophies of 2 great philosophers i.e. Kant and Hegel.

Antony C. Sutton, in one of his books entitled "The Order", explains: "From this system of Hegelian philosophy comes the historical dialectic i.e. that all historical events emerge from a **conflict** between opposing forces". End quote.

FACT 9 — The Gulf war was apparently an arranged war where both the U.S.A. through their ambassador, April C. Glaspie, and the Soviet Union through their ambassador, General Makashov, appeared to give conflicting advice to Saddam Hussein. (Whilst we were on one of our U.S. lecture tours, we viewed on t.v. the Congress questioning Ms Glaspie on the advice she gave to Iraq prior to the Gulf war.) Taking this advice that there would probably be no outside interference if he invaded Kuwait, meant that Saddam became a pawn in the hands of the New World Order people, and became the unwitting catalyst that launched the New World Order.

George Bush made this very clear in subsequent speeches where he explained that a combined world force was the first public display of unity under this New World Order.

This was the CONFLICT that initiated the plan. This

will now help you, the reader, to understand why the U.S. did not proceed to wipe out Saddam along with Iraq.

They brushed away the cobwebs but left the spider—Why?

Now, with this next phrase, I apologise to all patriotic Americans.

Those who fought in any way in the Gulf war, thought they were fighting to keep the world a free place, but in actuality, they fought the first battle under the title "New World Order" and in doing so, have helped in the:

(a) collapse of the sovereignty of the U.S.A
(b) plan to create massive unemployment
(c) plan to take away individual rights as guaranteed under the Constitution of the United States of America.

What Saddam Hussein really did was assist the New World Order leaders to serve a message to the whole world including Gadaffi of Libya, that any nation who in the future might be tempted to defy the international armies of the New World Order, would receive exactly the same ruthless treatment that was afforded to Saddam Hussein.

I repeat, "Why didn't they kill him?"

Because they may need Operation Desert Storm Part 2 or even an attack on Gadaffi and Libya to boost the President's popularity just prior to the elections in November 1992. (The media later scratched this attempt.)

STOP PRESS! 25 Nov. 1992. The U.S. elections are over and contrary to most expectations, (including those of this author), the NWO folk ditched George Bush and brought in their next man, Bill Clinton. Remember the OAITCCT (ie The Old Arsenic in the Coffee Cup Trick) can change things overnight. Ask Jack Kennedy.

33

Proof — New Zealand Herald, 5th November 1980 — "Websters in early for the last word".

"The Republic Challenger, Mr Ronald Reagan, has caused a major upset in the United States presidential election by beating Mr Jimmy Carter.

So, in effect, says the latest edition of Webster's dictionary, even though Americans do not go to the polls until later today to decide their president for the next four years . . .

Mr Reagan has been listed in the dictionary as the 40th president of the United States along with his 39 predecessors . . .

The presumption or genuine mistake by the Chicago publishers, . . . has dumbfounded the American consul-general in Auckland . . .

'Unbelievable', was his first word . . .

Auckland representatives of the publishers were just as surprised and had no explanations . . ." End quote.

Please remember both George Bush and Bill Clinton have been groomed by World Government groups and either would have done to complete the job started by Mr Bush.

FACT 10 — As we have pointed out already, the complete plan was so devious that the planners thought that not 1 in a million would ever work it out. Well, by the grace of God, we have done just that and these are our findings. In an article written many years back, we have a copy of their aims clearly outlined.

Quote: "Who will ever suspect then, that all these peoples were stage-managed by us according to a political plan which no one has so much as guessed at in the course of many centuries . . ." End quote. (See our book "Warning", page 80.)

FACT 11 — Using economy as a lever, the sovereignty of most nations on earth is being undermined.

Who are these World Government money lenders? You will need to concentrate very carefully at this point as the information is fairly heavy.

(a) Bank of International Settlements (BIS) — G7 — International Monetary Fund (IMF) and the World Bank etc, each of whom is involved in the New World Order, loaned massive amounts of money to countries around the world.

(b) Along with the loans, they inserted **CONDITIONALITIES POLICIES**, which meant "You will obey our conditions or you don't get the money".

e.g. If I were to lend money to any of my children to purchase a house, I would not be very happy if they went out and bought a yacht. To make sure that this did not take place, I would require that they sign a document stating that the money would be used for the correct purpose.

Furthermore, if I were a hard-nosed business man (which I am not), I would make very strong suggestions as to how this loan was to be repaid —

(1) they would take up extra employment such as working on petrol pumps or cleaning buildings at night in conjunction with their ordinary day-time jobs.

(2) any holidays they had due to them would be used working for money to pay back the original loan.

These two illustrations show the **meaning of CONDITIONALITIES POLICIES**.

(c) The United Nations, also connected with the New World Order, had secret meetings with the countries' leaders, where they persuaded each country to sign many, many, **international treaties** and agreements that were binding, **no matter which government was elected to run the country.**

FACT 12 — People all around the world today are asking the same question — "WHY DON'T THE POLITICIANS THAT WE ELECT TO PARLIAMENT OR CONGRESS KEEP THEIR ELECTION PROMISES??

Answer — THEY CAN'T!!

Why? — Because their policies have already been decided, signed and sealed, years ago by unwitting political dupes who preceded them to the halls of power.

Proof — From Antony Sutton's book 'The Order', page 119 we read: 'What then is the function of a Parliament or a Congress for Hegelians? (Author's note — Remember, Hegel was the German philosopher.)

THESE INSTITUTIONS ARE MERELY TO **ALLOW INDIVIDUALS TO FEEL** THAT THEIR OPINIONS HAVE SOME **VALUE** AND TO ALLOW A GOVERNMENT TO TAKE ADVANTAGE OF WHATEVER WISDOM THE 'PEASANT' MAY ACCIDENTALLY DEMONSTRATE.

As Hegel puts it BY VIRTUE OF THIS PARTICIPATION, SUBJECTIVE LIBERTY AND CONCEIT, INDIVIDUALS CAN SHOW THEMSELVES PALPABLY EFFICACIOUS AND **ENJOY THE SATISFACTION OF FEELING THEMSELVES TO COUNT FOR SOMETHING** . . ." End quote. (Capitals added for emphasis.)

So, from now on, please do not blame any politician for apparently lying to you. Many of them are sincere individuals who managed to get themselves elected.

99.9% of course would not have any idea of the way they were being manipulated.

If you, the ordinary citizen, has been confused, imagine if you can, how much more confusing it must be for those who are supposed to be in power. Not only confusing, but embarrassing!

I suppose what we really need is for all elected officials to be ordered to read this little booklet, then have a courageous leader stand up and publicly state:

"Citizens of . . . (insert your country's name), although I find these words difficult to utter, I feel obliged as an

honourable man to hereby publicly announce that we, your supposed democratically elected representatives **do not any longer in fact represent any of you.**

No one ever explained to us before in words easy to be understood that we are now part of a group calling itself NEW WORLD ORDER.

Our decisions on monetary matters, social welfare matters, energy matters, food matters, internal matters, external matters, are all being dictated to us.

Therefore, as it only takes about 20 of us to carry out the orders dictated to us by our masters, the rest of the parliamentarians, including the Opposition members have from this moment been made **REDUNDANT**. As they have just ceased their employment with us, we have invited them to make their way home using public transport at their own expense, of course.

We implore all of you involved in the work force to never again consider STRIKING if you are not satisfied with your living or working conditions. This was all right under the OLD ORDER but under the NEW ORDER, you simply lose your jobs forever. Therefore, don't do it!"

Proof—To those New Zealand citizens who remember the new Ferry attempting to start up between the North and South Islands of New Zealand during the months of April/May 1992, please note the then Prime Minister's words. He said "Picket lines and strikes were all right under the **old order**, but not viable any longer under the **NEW ORDER**." The reason for this being so, is that Unionism is finished for ever under the N.W.O.

It is obvious then that at least this man understood some of the rules.

FACT 13 — New Zealand and Australia were the world's first test case or guinea pigs for all these New World Order plans. (Proof — see page 135 in our book "Final Notice".)

The New Zealand voters thought that by voting out Party A and voting in Party B, the policies would change. They didn't of course, and the Minister of Finance under Party B, followed on with the wrecking policies of the Minister of Finance in Party A.

NOW DO YOU UNDERSTAND WHY?

New Zealand is the guinea pig nation! This is why we can afford to make authoratative statements.

FACT 14 — This author is a New Zealander by birth and can therefore, explain to readers in other countries what to expect.

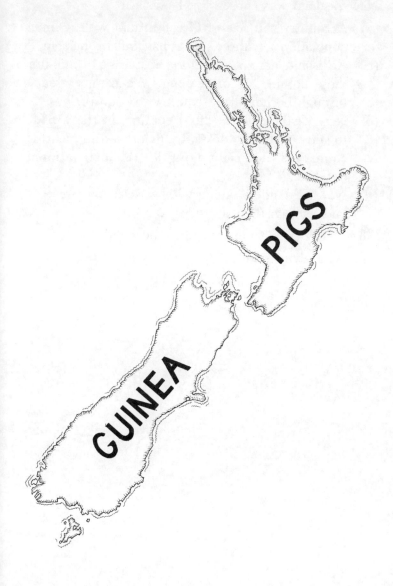

New Zealand was chosen for 4 reasons:

(a) A country the size of Great Britain with a small population i.e. three and a half million persons.

(b) An island nation, therefore, it is easy to monitor those coming in or leaving. We cannot escape through borders from country to country.

(c) **New Zealand is the "first country in the world" to start each new day's financial trading, as this country is sited right alongside the international dateline.**

(d) New Zealanders, along with Australians, are very laid back in their attitudes to life.

The New Zealand motto — "She'll be right".

The Australian motto — "She'll be right, mate".

PART THREE

HOW TO DESTROY A COUNTRY

FACT 15 — To keep the public's mind off what is really happening, take over the media and promote **RED HERRINGS** i.e. "apparent" global problems...

(a) Nuclear threat
(b) Greenhouse effect
(c) Ozone depletion
(d) Environmental issues
(e) Create new vocabulary e.g. Global Village, Nuclear Family, Environmentally Friendly.
     etc etc

Catch Words

(a) Restructuring — means destroying the old system completely.
(b) Redundant — (retrenchment) means getting the sack in three stages.
     Stage 1 — leak the news that it is going to happen.
     Stage 2 — deny that it is going to happen.
     Stage 3 — do it, sack them, or make it happen.
     This of course is a psychological ploy.
     Stage 1 — Shocks the worker into tears of disbelief.
     Stage 2 — The denial helps the shock wear off but the threat remains in the worker's mind.
     Stage 3 — "There. That wasn't so bad was it?"

(c) Pain — This term will be used by those who are in charge of the country's finances. They may even say "There is some belt-tightening to be done." It should be noted that these same people do not suffer any pain nor do their belts appear to require tightening.

(d) Light at the end of the tunnel — is such a jolly phrase. It certainly helps keep up the morale of the sufferers.

It is similar to the gas station proprietor who puts up a sign saying "Free gasoline tomorrow".

The next morning, cars are lined up for miles. As each car driver fuels up his vehicle, he has to pay, as the owner explains, "The operative word is **TOMORROW**".

FACT 16 — The New World Order people operate under the principles of **Fabian Socialism**.

There are three main planks which need to be borne in mind:

(a) GRADUALISM — sneak up on the people — at the right moment, hit hard and never deviate, otherwise all your waiting has been in vain!

Illustration — In New Zealand, the guinea-pig country, both ministers of finance from Party A and Party B were asked to slow down with their restructuring. They both refused even though it meant POLITICAL SUICIDE. The New World Order leaders can always reward them quietly, later on of course.

(b) DISPOSSESSION — Separate the land and property from the owner as ownership of land gives one a measure of security which is not permitted under the New World Order.

Methods used — tax, tax, tax. Rates rise continually. Finally the owner cannot pay. He signs the land over to its new owners i.e. the New World Order people through their money-lenders, and becomes a tenant on his own property.

Illustration — In late 1991 whilst conducting meetings in the North Island of New Zealand, I was approached by a man at the conclusion of the meeting who advised me that an orchardist nearby had just had this very scenario happen to him.

(c)   PAUPERISATION — means to destroy each sector of society using the best methods possible.

e.g. ruined sectors in New Zealand and Australia.

WATCH THIS HAPPEN TO YOUR COUNTRY!
Take a pen and check off each event.

(1) Merge County Councils and small committees. This is called Centralisation. Get rid of local government using mergers.   ( )

(2) Create continuous change in every area. This brings about the necessary confusion to implement the New World Order.   ( )

(3) Transport ruined through continual taxation and charges.   ( )

(4) Farmers ruined.   ( )

At this time of writing, newswatchers will have noticed that the European farmers are now under attack by the NWO policies and as I said years ago in our public meetings, these people will not take it lying down as New Zealand and Australian farmers did. It is of note that once the subsidies began to be removed from these European farmers, their protests were very loud and strident e.g. burning trucks, dumping fish on the steps of the European Community headquarters in Brussels and eggs being thrown at politicians, are merely a few of their antics.

(5) Business ruined in farm related towns.   ( )

(6) Education ruined.   ( )

45

(7) Fish quotas ruin private operators.   ( )
(8) Tax all animals on the hoof.   ( )
(9) Plant Breeders Right (P.B.R.) — turn seeds into
    hybrids.   ( )
(10) Health — subsidised medical treatment and medicines
     stopped.   ( )
(11) Hospitals and nursing — massive staff cuts and shut
     downs.   ( )
(12) Pharmacies being closed down.   ( )
(13) Post Offices being closed down all over the country.
                                                        ( )
(14) Communications must be transformed ready for a
     Global Communications Network with a Global
     dossier on every individual.   ( )
(15) Senior Citizens Superannuation must be attacked.
                                                        ( )
(16) Phone booths change colour. No more cash in
     phones. All card phones.   ( )
(17) Plastic cards for electricity users.   ( )

Here are the New World Order Rules in part:

(a) By controlling energy, we can control nations.
(b) By controlling food, we can control individuals.
(c) All small businesses must be destroyed but at the
     same time, the charade continues as a pretence is
     made of helping small businesses.
(d) All big business must MERGE, MERGE,
     MERGE, until about 6 major companies control
     each individual country. These companies will set
     up giant supermarkets and shopping malls selling
     everything from a pin to a motor car.

To help to destroy all individuality and small business,
VAT, GST (Goods and Services Tax) or Consumption
Tax, must be introduced to each country. This becomes

a nightmare in book-keeping for the small business man who ultimately can't stand the strain and allows his business to collapse.

Through computerisation, this type of tax sets up a SPY SYSTEM where all are caught in the net operated by your friendly tax man.

N.B. Woe betide countries like Greece and Italy when they bring in this form of taxation. Their prisons will be literally packed with tax dodgers who up until this stage have operated two sets of books and done all cash deals.

PART FOUR

WHAT TO EXPECT IN 1992

FACT 17 — New Zealand is in for a currency change, designed of course to catch drug dealers and money launderers, we are told.

(Notice the blank space left on all your new notes when the currency changes. Why is this? Is it possible there is to be a unified world logo to be placed on every nation's currencies?)

However, the reasons given to us for all these changes are never the true reasons for the changes. This is an important point to remember when dealing with these devious characters.

FACT 18 — The United States of America was, until recently, in for a currency change. This has not yet taken place, which fact is mystifying those in the know. Possibly it will not take place until after the elections, or again the N.W.O. people may decide to cancel cash more quickly and move straight on to the Smart Card with a computer built in. This would lead on of course to the microchip under the flesh.

If the currency did change, the one note that would not be altered "of course" would be the $1 bill with the occult, Satanic, Masonic seals on the reverse side.

FACT 19 — The Swiss banks are moving against money laundering.

Newspaper cutting dated 11th May 1991 — Quote: ". . . the Federal Banking Commission (EBK) announced that Switzerland was abolishing most of its anonymous bank accounts to crack down on criminal transactions.

Form B accounts which preserved anonymity by allowing bank clients to conduct all bank transactions through a lawyer, notary or trust administrator, have become a notorious cover for money-laundering by drugs runners and corrupt dictators.

Existing Form B accounts will have to be replaced by a written statement on **THE IDENTITY OF THE REAL OWNER BY SEPTEMBER 30 1992 AT THE LATEST**, the EBK said in a statement." End quote. Emphasis added.

FACT 20 — **The Earth Summit** took place in Rio de Janeiro, Brazil from 1-12 June 1992. Under the umbrella of the United Nations, they hoped this would be the LARGEST GATHERING OF HEADS OF STATE AND GOVERNMENTS IN HISTORY.

The man in charge was Maurice Strong, a very influential New Age advocate well known in the U.S. through the setting up of the BACA, a New Age centre in Colorado.

This man tried to buy up water rights in one section of Colorado, but there was a local outcry and he failed in his bid. These New World Order people really mean business.

Another interesting speaker at this conference was to be Ronald Biggs, the big train robber, who was to speak on the subject of "crime". Mr Biggs is ideally suited to this subject of course.

Under the Greenies banner, these persons will ultimately con the majority of World citizens into the worship of the Earth Goddess GAIA which is connected with the Feminist movement.

Aims of this World Conference: To have each nation on earth yield up some of its HERITAGE NATURE AREAS to be controlled by an international body — clever? yes, diabolically so!

On the 23rd of May 1992, we were viewing the National news in Melbourne, Australia. A mass of protesters gathered on that day in the middle of the city, to register their anger at the proposed government plan to lock up 21 wilderness areas from the general public. Four wheel drive club members and others were there. Cattle men and deer hunters were there too!

I chuckled as the Government spokesman assured them that all would be well. If only this book had been ready for distribution. Link this news with the earth Summit to be held in Rio de Janiero in June 1992 and learn to say goodbye to your wilderness areas as their ownership travels overseas.

The world media latched on to the Rio Earth Conference with great vigour and zest. Important figures such as Maurice Strong, Shirley Maclaine and the Dalai Lama appeared on television from time to time.

One shock for us all was to observe the ex-leader of the U.S.S.R. i.e. Mikhail Gorbachev being elevated to his new position **"President of the Green Cross"**.

Meaning:

— the Red Cross looks after sick people

— the Green Cross looks after a sick environment

Notice that as Communism **appeared** to collapse, Gorbachev and Bush were the best of friends, smiling and being photographed together, along with their wives.

Newswatchers will have noted that one large and significant nation has refused to sign the Biodiversity Treaty (which means the protection of endangered species of flora and fauna) i.e. the United States of America.

Why? With the U.S. elections coming up, George Bush cannot openly side with the greenie movement. He made this quite clear when he said the New World Order is not connected in any way to the environmental movement.

Author's comment — The reason for this is clear. The electorate is made up of greenies and non-greenies. The non-greenie voters would be in the majority.

Loggers are losing their jobs in the Washington state so that the spotted owl can continue in its natural habitat. As a result, one of these disgruntled loggers put up a sign by the highway —

"I love the spotted owl — fried!"

The greenie movement has not been around for very long. It was obviously **discovered** as being a very powerful tool to influence people all around the world into seeking global co-operation.

Author's note — The environmental (greenie) movement is being used by the New World Order people to attain their ends.

A Green Bank

An environmental conference was held in Denver, Colorado, at the end of the decade of the 80's. A Christian friend of ours managed to attend this meeting and to his surprise, he saw a number of people present whom you would not expect to be at such a conference. These men represented the financial aristocracy. Names such as Rockefeller, Rothschilds and Maurice Strong were in attendance.

The discussions were supposed to be highly secret but I have in my possession a tape recording of one of these sessions where they discussed setting up **A GREEN BANK** connected with the Royal Bank of Canada in Montreal.

I was shocked when one of the delegates made this statement **"We must keep this information from the cannon fodder that unfortunately populates the earth."**

Presumably, both I and you the reader, have been relegated to this class.

The idea was presented that a global message was to go out that all banks were becoming unreliable and subject to financial collapse. Therefore, investors and those seeking mortgages for land and real-estate, should invest in the green bank.

Once these transactions had been completed, then the green bank would suffer a "supposed" major breakdown, the loans for the mortgages would be called in and the majority of borrowers of course would not have the ready cash to do this. Their properties would then become owned by the green bank.

In these days, in the light of all this deception taking place, it is more important to have a personal relationship to the Creator than to try and protect His creation!

The sad fact is that once these ends have been achieved, these environmental (greenie) pawns will be ridiculed as being no longer useful. It has been sad to observe them collecting smiles and playing up to the media. This has been their temporary moment of glory.

FACT 21 — The European Community comes to power on the 31st December 1992. This is the final World Empire which will control all Global Trade for a short season. Borders will be dissolved, national sovereignty will give way to INTERNATIONALISM and this will lead on to THE CASHLESS SOCIETY then THE MARK OF THE BEAST SYSTEM.

Media watchers will have noticed no doubt that the Eastern European countries (which can never become full members of the European Community as they are geographically in the wrong position according to article 237 of the European Communities Act) will link, in many cases, as associate members (n.b. page 18 in our book "Warning" written in 1980.)

It has been fascinating to watch the rise of Roman Catholicism in many of these countries, filling a religious vacuum that came about through atheistic communism. (Evangelical Christians thankfully are also moving into this area with the true gospel of the Lord Jesus Christ.) In prophecy the city of Rome i.e. the city founded on the seven hills, plays a prominent part together with the political European Community in these days.

All around the world today, national armies are undergoing massive changes and being radically depleted. Army camps are closing down, and the purpose of course, is as follows.

A global village where we all live together in harmony as brothers and sisters no longer requires each country to have their own military forces. Therefore, there will very shortly be formed:

A Global Army

In Germany, at this time of writing, there is an army being formed which is mystifying observers. Many are asking, "What is the purpose of this army, how big will it become and how soon will it be until it takes the place of all existing armies?"

FACT 22 — SUMMARY — THE NEW WORLD ORDER means:

No personal freedoms
No religious freedom
No right to own your own home
No right to own your own children
No right to run your own business
No right to hold your own beliefs at all
God becomes the earth and the Cosmos
The TRUE GOD as a separate creator has no place

PART FIVE

HOW IT WILL BE DONE

FACT 23 — The letters NIEO probably do not mean much to you. They stand for NEW INTERNATIONAL ECONOMIC ORDER i.e. a cashless society.

STAGES — The Japanese economy depends on its REAL ESTATE PRICES. A five minute **earthquake** in **Tokyo** could set all this in motion.

(a)   The Japanese Real Estate prices must fall, then on to a Stock Market Crash in Japan. This in turn will collapse the U.S. dollar and the German Mark. The whole world economy will collapse overnight.

(b)   Everybody who wishes to buy or sell will be given a PLASTIC CARD — a combination credit and debit card.

(c)   There are at least 7 problems with the plastic card. They can be:

    (1)   Broken — they snap in half easily.

    (2)   Lost — imagine yourself on an overseas trip and you lose your card.

    (3)   Stolen — professional criminals are having a ball already.

    (4)   Wiped — by passing a magnet over the strip
               — by leaving two cards face to face
               — by leaving your card in the sunlight

(5) Bent — by leaving your card in a rounded wallet
(6) The carbon copy of one of your card transactions can be stolen and mail ordering done over the telephone using your number.
(7) In Hong Kong, criminals are duplicating the cards.

FACT 24 — This brings us to a very important prophecy which is in the process right now of being fulfilled. Written in 96 A.D., on an island called Patmos in the Aegean Sea, by a man called simply "John". It refers to two great world leaders who will appear on the world scene shortly.

i.e. One   WORLD   GOVERNMENT — Leader — **Antichrist** (Beast)

One WORLD RELIGION — Leader — **False Prophet**

Both of these will be controlled by a supernatural being — **Lucifer** (Satan) i.e. the Eye in the triangle on the reverse side of every U.S. $1 bill since 1933.

Highly important fact—

Never let any person seriously think that the eye of the triangle is the eye of the God of the Christians. Those in the occult will recognise it immediately as the **illuminated eye** of Lucifer (Satan).

Prophecy:

"And he causeth all both small and great, rich and poor, free and bond, to receive a mark in their right hand or in their foreheads. And that no man might buy or sell, save he that had the mark, or the name of the beast, or the number of his name.

Here is wisdom. Let him that hath understanding count the number of the beast, for it is the number of a man and his number is

six hundred	= 6
three score	= 6
and six	= 6

FACT 25—Every person in New Zealand and Australia, and shortly the whole world system connected with the E.C., will be on the computers under a 666 system.

Birthdate—If you were born on July 7th 1977, your computer number will be: 77 (year) 07 (month) 07 (day).

Location—Satellite cameras have enabled the New World Order people to photograph the whole world along with cities and towns. i.e. **Mesh block**—

Large block—city—02
Medium block—area—47

Small block—to within two streets—11

=Thus your location would be 024711.

I.D.—All countries are being forced through the CONDITIONALITIES POLICIES AND INTERNATIONAL TREATIES to give each of their citizens an I.D.

HOW IT IS DONE.

(a) Leak the news to the media that I.D. cards are to be introduced.

(b) Furious debate takes place—marches etc, submissions accepted.

(c) Ignore all opinions, give everybody an I.D.—It has already been decided.

During the year 1991, we were holding meetings in Fiji and were invited to speak to Members of the Cabinet of the Interim Government at a special breakfast which was arranged. I spoke to them about the New World Order and as I was about to conclude my remarks, mentioned that very shortly, they, as parliamentarians would be forced to give every person in their country an I.D.

The whole scenario appeared to be very strange, as here I stood, instructing the so-called legislators and rule-makers as to what they or their colleagues would be doing in the future. Remember, this I.D. will be forced upon you also in the days ahead. It is a World Government plan.

e.g. I.D. no. 437121

Now again in order:

Birthdate—770707

Location —024711

I.D. —437121

By using LINK NUMBERS, all computer dossiers can readily be brought together.

59

FACT 26 — The SILICON CHIP is already being used in animals — dogs, cats, fish, birds, horses etc.

In the t.v. programme BEYOND 2000, it has been suggested that gangs in New York and other cities are on the agenda and then on to jail-inmates, and later to all who will receive it. Clever psychological advertising of course will be the norm.

MICRO-DOT IMPLANT

The Japanese have spent years updating the silicon chip and have now come up with a tiny dot observable only under a microscope and no doubt this, or an up-dated version, will be used as the mark of the beast system. Yuppies and others who have been psychologically conned, will be the first to line up for the privilege of receiving this **micro-dot implant.**

This micro-dot will certainly be a more attractive proposition than a glass tube full of electronic equipment being placed under your flesh.

OUR FIRM ADVICE — Use the plastic card system by all means, but NEVER RECEIVE THE MARK ON YOUR BODY. You would then become a walking piece of currency. Whoever controls the world economy will then control you.

The Australian Government because of the conditionalities policies foisted on them by the New World Order money lenders, initially aimed to give every Australian citizen an I.D. number.

One man thought up a plan to defeat this I.D. system being implemented. The average citizen laughed at this **apparent victory** and said, "We beat them that time." Not really. These guys are so sneaky that they had a contingency plan up their sleeve — **T.F.N.** A **"Tax File Number"** was later introduced.

(a) It was not compulsory — good news.

(b) You couldn't conduct any business or economic deal without it — bad news.

Prepare for the Shocking Info.

May and I were in Australia on a lecture tour during the month of May 1992. A letter was passed on to us with the following information:

All employees were told to give their T.F.N. to their pay offices (for the first time.) This man refused to do this, so he was informed that he would be required to pay his tax at the HIGHEST RATE. He agreed to do this.

When he received his next group certificate, look at the T.F.N. they gave him — 666-666-666. I have a copy of his form before me as I write. This is **not** a story from a friend of a friend of a friend.

Although this man was not a Christian, he knew it to be the devil's number. The pay office told him it is just a code they use for the computer to show who has not given their tax file number.

When I spoke this out in a public meeting, a man told me later that it made his skin crawl.

A girl who worked for an accountant called out in one of our public meetings that she had seen this 666-666-666 before. Further confirmation indeed.

STOP PRESS!

Just prior to going to print, we guinea pig New Zealanders, have a further item of interest to pass on to readers around the world.

TRAPPED IN YOUR OWN HOME!

Interest rates have suddenly been lowered, and numbers

of our friends and acquaintances have been invited by their friendly bankers to refinance their existing loans to cover additional luxuries such as an extra room on the house, a boat or a caravan etc.

WARNING — Remember how the World Government financiers took over and destroyed nations? They used exactly the same principles.

(a) Issue low interest rate loans with attractive repayment clauses.

(b) Put up the interest rates.

(c) Foreclose.

To all homeowners who are considering refinancing, remember the following:

(a) Make sure you retain at least 51% equity in your property at all times.

(b) Bear in mind that the World Government people have plans already formulated to devalue the world real estate market as soon as possible after the U.S. elections in November 1992.

(c) This devaluation will raise the equity that the lending establishments have in householders' properties in many cases to over 100%. People will then become discouraged and any householders caught in this dreadful position would naturally try to quickly sell their home to recoup their losses. However, as the house could well be worth less than the value of the mortgage, they are trapped into either staying in their home and paying off the original mortgage or walking away and forcing a mortgagee sale.

Remember that those who choose to stay and pay off their original mortgage will find that the interest rates will be raised higher and higher so that they cannot afford to meet the repayments each month and will find themselves in the same position as the others.

(e) To those who find this concept difficult to receive, take note that the Westpac bank in Australia went down to the tune of 2 billion dollars in the month of May 1992. This was purely the result of a drop in real estate prices of commercial properties.

This author has read most of the literature on world government plans.

One of the first aims of each group has been to separate the land from the owner and the owner from the land.

Reason—**ownership of land gives one a measure of security** which is not deemed necessary by the New World leaders.

Here is an antidote to fear brought on by reading the above section.

PART SIX

WHAT TO DO.

By now you will have realised that contrary to what most believe, things are not going to get better. We all need a strong spiritual base for our lives at this point. At the end of this book we have outlined a prayer which needs to be prayed by every thinking person.

There is a strong commitment to be made, firstly to your Creator who made you, and then to His Son, the Lord Jesus Christ, who died for your sins.

This Christian life we recommend is not the one portrayed on television showing a man with a dog collar and nanny glasses drinking cups of tea with elderly ladies.

It is rather a vital, covenant relationship entered into and enjoyed by, both the Lord God and the individual. The result of this covenant will be the discovery that there are millions of others world wide who have gladly embraced this new birth experience.

Settle for nothing less!

WHAT OPTIONS DO I HAVE?—*Past the Point of No Return!*

We can clearly see by now that we all have quite a problem.

FACT — No longer is this problem POLITICAL, RELIGIOUS OR ECONOMIC — IT IS DIABOLIC-ALLY SATANIC AND THEREFORE, SPIRITUAL.

PROOF — At this point, please turn back to the strange seal with the eye in the triangle. Do not attempt to sidestep the issue. No amount of bluster on your part will change the situation one iota.

FACT — The Great God who made the world and all that is in it provided a text book for life.

The 666 prophecy being fulfilled so clearly in our generation was predicted in detail in the year 96 A.D. Revelation 13:16-18.

Now, in the same book of prophecy we observe the gracious advice of a caring Creator, that we turn to Him with all our hearts.

FACT — There is a book in God's library called the "Lamb's Book of Life".

RULES

(a)   Anybody whose name is in that book will not receive the demonic mark of the Beast on their body.

Revelation 13:8 — "And all that dwell upon the earth shall worship him, whose names are not written in the book of life of the Lamb slain from the foundation of the world."

They will be miraculously provided for by a supernatural God during these difficult days. They belong to the Lord and as such, are promised His special care during this time.

A TRUE STORY

In the year 1962, my wife May and I were living in the Island of Western Samoa. I had just finished reading a book on the life of George Mueller of Bristol and had been impressed with the story of this man of prayer. I read how that for fifty years he had collected orphans from the streets in Bristol, England and had set them up in orphanages, relying only on the Lord to supply every need.

I quote from "George Mueller — Man of Faith":

"You have always found the Lord faithful to His promise, Mr Mueller?"

"Always! He has never failed me! For nearly seventy years every need in connection with this work has been supplied. The orphans from the first until now have numbered nine thousand five hundred, but they have never wanted a meal. Hundreds of times we have commenced the day without a penny, but our Heavenly Father has sent supplies the moment they were actually required. There never was a time when we had no wholesome meal. During all these years I have been enabled to trust in the living God alone. In answer to prayer $7,500,000 have been sent to me."

I well remember the Sunday when I told May that I had invited Pastor Makisua Fatialofa and his wife Mau for lunch. She mentioned that we had no food. I replied that I had just finished reading George Mueller's book and that all would be well.

We duly sat at the table and I asked Pastor Fatialofa to give thanks for our dinner, mentioning at the same time that there was nothing to eat. With a little smile about his lips, he thanked the Lord and as soon as he said the word "amen", we heard a knock at the door.

I jumped to my feet and said "Just like the book". Opening the door, I saw a large cardboard box packed with hot steaming food — taros, bananas, chop suey, chickens, meat, coconut cream, luau, was all there. I didn't wait for one moment. I ran past the box and out in to the back yard, then around the sides of the house, then to the road. There was no sign of any person, no dust that a car would have stirred up, and certainly no time for anybody to run away and hide.

This is my statement — **We have been fed by an angel!**"

Some will reply at this stage — "I do not believe this to be the case". This does not concern me at all as we ate the food and you didn't.

(b) Anybody who takes this mark of the Beast will temporarily be able to buy and sell, but will finish up in Hell or the Lake of Fire forever. They will never come out.

God's forever is FOREVER!

Revelation 14:9-11 — "And the third angel followed them, saying with a loud voice, If any man worship the beast and his image, and receive his mark in his forehead, or in his hand,

The same shall drink of the wine of the wrath of God, which is poured out without mixture into the cup of his indignation; and he shall be tormented with fire and brimstone in the presence of the holy angels, and in the presence of the Lamb:

And the smoke of their torment ascendeth up forever and ever: and they have no rest day nor night, who worship the beast and his image, and whosoever receiveth the mark of his name."

FACT — Why do people have to go to Hell for receiving a simple microdot in their flesh?

Answer — Your forehead is reserved for the Name of your Creator and Manufacturer. If you receive the mark of his arch-enemy, there will be no room there for His Name.

Revelation 22:4 refers to the Name of our Lord Jesus Christ — our manufacturer — "And they shall see His face and His Name shall be in their foreheads."

You choose — God or Satan
Heaven or Hell
God's Book or Satan's Hit List

Barry Smith — I'M TERRIFIED! DO YOU HAVE ANY GOOD NEWS?

YES!

(a) Politics has failed you.
(b) Religion will fail you.
(c) Economy will fail you.
(d) Friends will fail you.
(e) **CHRIST** will **not** fail you.

Many years ago, a man called John Wesley rode or led his horse through the English countryside. As he traversed the country, he would regularly quote this very deep thought — "I am a spirit come from God. I am a spirit going to God."

William Shakespeare said "All the world's a stage and we are merely players. We enter on one side, play our part and then leave from the other side." (Paraphrase.)

Billy Graham, the great evangelist, has said "This life is but a dressing room for the next. This is not the final act."

During the month of May 1992, my wife May and I were on a lecture tour of South Australia and Victoria. On the final night of our South Melbourne meetings, we arrived

68

at the hall only to view the masses of cars and people pouring in to take up every available space.

Out on the main highway two flashing red lights signalled that all was not well. May and I ran across and to our horror, observed the body of an elderly lady lying on the road. Her husband Arthur, sat quietly in the gutter nearby.

May and I went across and sat by him. He told us that they had travelled about 100 miles to attend this final meeting. They were strong believers in the Lord and were running late because they had been counselling someone else in need.

Twenty minutes later, I was on the platform preparing to speak whilst May and others took Arthur into an office nearby and provided him with hot drinks. This dear man was determined to stay at the meeting as he made it clear that this was the reason he and his wife had come.

I continued on with my message for two hours as I normally do, and knowing Arthur could hear every word I spoke, I called out "Arthur, listen to this —

'For the Lord Himself shall descend from heaven with a shout, with the voice of the archangel, and the trump of God, and the dead in Christ shall rise first'".

I interjected "Arthur, this is where your dear wife Rita will stand up on her feet." I continued the quote —

"Then we which are alive and remain, shall be caught up together with them in the clouds to meet the Lord in the air and so shall we ever be with the Lord."

I interjected again — "Arthur, this is where you come into the picture. At this point, you will join Rita once again and be miraculously caught up to meet Jesus in the clouds." I then completed the quote —

"Wherefore, comfort one another with these words!"

As is my custom, at the end of the message, I gave the invitation to the 1300 strong audience present to come to the front of the hall and make a calculated, clear, public, decision to live out the rest of their days for God and the Lord and Saviour, Jesus Christ.

As the people began to move, there stood dear Arthur along side my wife May and others who had come forward, with his arms raised to heaven, worshipping the Lord that he and Rita had loved and served for so many years.

The presence of God was so strong that night that in thirty years of travelling the world, never before have I known a feeling like it. I marvelled that a man who had just lost his wife two hours before, could stand publicly as Arthur did that night.

No wonder the greenies are all upset. Without this vital relationship with God through the Lord Jesus Christ, these people only have a past and a present and certainly no future. Is it any wonder then that they are desperately trying to hold on to what they have in the form of this world and its resources.

Are you aware that Jesus Christ is coming back again?
He is coming back for those who are prepared for His return.
It is possible for you to know that you are one of these.
This is a very short explanation of future events.
I have done my best.
This is enough.
It is now up to you.

CALVARY

On one of our earlier trips to Israel and the Middle East, our tour party stayed at the Pilgrim's Palace Hotel just outside the wall of Jerusalem.

70

May and I were ushered to our bedroom which faced the Arab bus station, and just beyond that a strangely shaped hill with holes in its side like two eye sockets and one for the mouth. This we knew to be the place where God sent His Son to pay the price for all sin.

Can you imagine the thrill of waking up morning by morning, pulling back the curtains, and viewing the very site where your sins, and my sins, were paid for in full through the precious blood of the Lord Jesus Christ.

Some may wonder why I would include this section at the conclusion of a book of this nature.

My answer would have to be, "Without this wonderful event being explained, the information in this book is completely useless as it simply tickles the intellect."

The fact is that the God who gave us all this prophetic information, also tells us that we are sinners in need of a Saviour—God has made provision for our salvation, but it is we who make the choice.

As a boy I learnt this verse—John 3:16:

"For God so loved the world that He gave His only begotten Son, that whosoever believeth in Him should not perish but have everlasting life."

It is obvious to anybody with any intellect at all, that although the price has been paid for all, not all are saved. There is a choice to be made.

YOUR DECISION FOR THE LORD JESUS CHRIST.

In our 30 years of touring the world, we have used a prayer at the end of every lecture that puts people into vital communication with God through Jesus Christ.

71

(1) Recognising that I am a sinner, who has strayed away from God, I now turn in His direction. I **REPENT** (with godly sorrow and remorse) from my self-willed lifestyle.

(2) I **BELIEVE** that if I was the last person on earth, Jesus Christ the Lord would have died for me, because He loved me so much — HIS PRECIOUS BLOOD COVERS MY SINS.

(3) At this very moment, I make my peace with God in a covenant agreement — I **RECEIVE** the Lord Jesus Christ into my life to be my own personal Saviour.

Here is the sinner's prayer:

Say out loud "Lord Jesus Christ, I come to you now, because I am a sinner.

Today, Lord Jesus, I repent of my sin, I turn away from my sin and I turn to you.

I believe dear Lord, that you died for me (insert your name) . . . I thank you dear Lord, because **your precious blood** covers all my sins. No one else can save me, only Jesus.

Right now, I open the door to my heart (put your hand to your chest and open outwards). Come into my heart Lord Jesus. Wash me, cleanse me, and make me your child. I receive you now by faith.

Help me to live for you every day until you come back again.

I close the door (use your hand again, bring it back towards your chest) and Jesus is inside.

I thank you Lord Jesus, because today, by faith, I have received you and **you have received me**.

Amen."

HERE IS THE PROMISE:

"To as many (anybody) as received Him (Jesus), to them gave He power to become the Sons of God." John 1:12. (Emphasis added).

Your choice this day gives you that power, and right, to call yourself a son of God—Praise Him now in your own words.

Please fill in the certificate on the back page and then:

1. Copy it out again into the front page of your Bible.
2. Send another copy to me immediately so that I can send you further assistance.
3. Go and tell someone what you have done.

"That if thou shalt **confess** with thy **MOUTH**, the Lord Jesus, and shalt **believe** in thine **HEART** that God has raised Him from the dead, thou shalt be **saved**." Romans 10:9. (Emphasis added).

That which is in your heart must come out of your mouth.

This is your starting point.

Now: Steps to help you continue on for Christ.

1. Pray daily.
2. Read your Bible daily. Start in John's Gospel, because it speaks about salvation and everlasting life.
3. Witness, or tell others about Christ.
4. Link up with a Bible-based Christian group or Church. Advise the Pastor of the fellowship of your decision and ask him to help you in your new Christian life.

WELCOME TO THE FAMILY OF GOD.

I look forward to meeting you up there.

Your friend,
Barry Smith.

NEW BIRTH CERTIFICATE

At . . . . .on . . . .
  (Time)   (Date)

I . . . .
                        (Name)

received the Lord Jesus Christ as my own Saviour. I thank
Him.

Signed . . . .

ADDITIONAL MATERIAL BY INTERNATIONAL SUPPORT MINISTRIES— (PACIFIC)

formerly Barry Smith Family Evangelism

Books:

"Warning" by Barry R. Smith
"Second Warning" by Barry R. Smith
"Final Notice" by Barry R. Smith

Music Cassettes:

"Trials of Your Faith" by Andrew and Saskia Smith
"Hidden Man of the Heart" by Andrew and Saskia Smith
"If My People" by Andrew and Saskia Smith
"The Secret Place" by Mark Baker and Andrew and Saskia Smith
Regular new releases.

Video Cassettes:

"The Monetary Crash'	(2 hours)
"Antichrist and the World Government"—Part 1	(2 hours)
—Part 2	(2 hours)
"Daniel 9—How Long Have We Got?"	(2 hours)
"The Occult and New Age Movement"	(2 hours)
"After Death—WHAT?"	(2 hours)
"Scarlet Woman—One World Church"	(2 hours)
"Chaos of the Cults"	(2 hours)
"Christian Family Series"	(3 videos—total of 6 hours)

Stock may be limited so please write for current catalogue and price list.

To order, please write to:

International Support Ministries—(Pacific)
Pelorus Bridge
Rai Valley
Marlborough
NEW ZEALAND
Phone no: (03) 571 6046; Fax no: (03) 571 6135

Barry Smith Family Evangelism
P.O. Box 94
Kurrajong
N.S.W. 2758
AUSTRALIA
Phone no: (045) 761 201; Fax no: (045) 761 488

Alpha Omega Ministries U.K.
Suite 1, 1st Floor
Mill Court
Newport
Isle of Wight
P030 2AA
ENGLAND
Phone no: (0983) 525 503; Fax no: (0983) 525 503

Ben Naude & Nic Venter
International Support Ministries (SA)
Montagu House,
Cnr Rivonia and North Roads,
Rivonia,
P.O.Box 1177,
Rivonia 2128,
South Africa.
Ph: (011) 803 6030; Fax: (011) 803 6031

OXYGEN THERAPIES

The book entitled 'Oxygen Therapies' by Ed McCabe, may be obtained by writing to:

Energy Publications, 99/RD1, Morrisville, NY 13408, U.S.A.

In this book from page 188 onwards, you may read of people and places using oxygenation. As Mr McCabe does not want any part of this book to be reproduced, we feel to honour his request and merely pass on a list of people and places using oxygenation.

We do this because people are desperate and in some cases do not have the time to go writing letters all around the world.

As we are not medically qualified to make any judgements about any of these clinics, or individuals administering oxygen therapy, the reader must exercise his or her own discretion in this matter.

Mexico and Germany

Gerson Institute Clinics c/o POB 430-OT, Bonita, CA 92002.

Donsbach Rosarita Beach Clinic c/o 323-OT E, San Ysidro Blvd, San Ysidro, CA 92073, U.S.

Kellner Clinic, Baden Weiler, Federal Republic of Germany.

Rosarita Beach Clinic—Ph: (706) 689 4465 or 619 426 2002.

Alexander Preuss, D-700 Stuttgart 1 (West), Bebel Strasse 29, Federal Republic of Germany.

"Dr Horst Kief—it has been alleged that he has cured a number of AIDS victims by drawing blood, infusing it with ozone and returning it to the patient at regular intervals until all the virus is gone. His address is: Biozon Ozon-technik GmbH, An Der Haune ffl10, Bad Hersfeld, D-6430, FEDERAL REPUBLIC OF GERMANY.

Dr S. Rilling of Stuttgart and Dr Renate Viebahn of Iffezhein are among the growing number of physicians who have obtained similar results with their patients. They are with Arztlich Gesellschaft fur Ozontherapie and J Hanslwer GmbH, respectively." (This excerpt is taken from "Health and Healing", Vol 8, No.1, October-December 1988.)

Recommended Reading

"The Energy Grid" by Bruce Cathie, P.O. Box 986, Tehachapi, Ca 93581, U.S.A. Ph: (805) 822 9655 Fax: (805) 822 9658.

Tapes and Books from William Campbell Douglas M.D.: Hydrogen Peroxide Manuscript $US9.95; The Cancer Cure that Worked (Book) $US13.95; Video Tape on Aids by Dr Douglas $US39.95; Video Tape on Aids by Dr Strecker $US35.00. Available from: P.O. Box 1568, Clayton, Georgia, 30525, U.S.A.